C

BEGINNING
TO
READ

HOUGHTON MIFFLIN LITERARY READERS

HOUGHTON MIFFLIN COMPANY   BOSTON

Atlanta   Dallas   Geneva, Illinois   Palo Alto   Princeton   Toronto

Program Authors

William K. Durr, John J. Pikulski, Rita M. Bean, J. David Cooper, Nicholas A. Glaser, M. Jean Greenlaw, Hugh Schoephoerster, Mary Lou Alsin, Kathryn Au, Rosalinda B. Barrera, Joseph E. Brzeinski, Ruth P. Bunyan, Jacqueline C. Comas, Frank X. Estrada, Robert L. Hillerich, Timothy G. Johnson, Pamela A. Mason, Joseph S. Renzulli

Senior Consultants

Jacqueline L. Chaparro, Alan N. Crawford, Alfredo Schifini, Sheila Valencia

Program Reviewers

Donna Bessant, Mara Bommarito, Yetive Bradley, Patricia M. Callan, Clara J. Hanline, Fannie Humphery, Barbara H. Jeffus, Beverly Jimenez, Sue Cramton Johnson, Michael P. Klentschy, Petra Montante, Nancy Rhodes, Julie Ryan, Lily Sarmiento, Ellis Vance, Judy Williams, Leslie M. Woldt, Janet Gong Yin

Acknowledgments

For each of the selections listed below, grateful acknowledgment is made for permission to adapt and/or reprint original or copyrighted material, as follows:

"Happiness," from *When We Were Very Young* by A.A. Milne. Copyright 1924 by E.P. Dutton, renewed 1952 by A.A. Milne. Reprinted by permission of the publisher, E.P. Dutton (a division of NAL Penguin, Inc.) and the Canadian publishers McClelland and Stewart, Toronto.

"My New Boy," by Joan Phillips, illustrated by Lynn Munsinger. Copyright © 1986 by Joan Phillips. Illustrations copyright © 1986 by Lynn Munsinger. Reprinted by permission of Random House, Inc.

"Pumpkin Pumpkin," entire text and some art from the book by Jeanne Titherington. Copyright © 1986 by Jeanne Titherington. Reprinted by permission of Greenwillow Books (a division of William Morrow).

"Water is Wet," by Penny Pollock, text copyright © 1985 by Penny Pollock. Reprinted by permission of G.P. Putnam's Sons.

Credits

Illustrators: 4–5 Roni Shepherd **6–17** Jeanne Titherington **18–27** James Marshall **44** Meg Kelleher **45–53** David McPhail **54–70** Lynn Munsinger **71–79** Marc Brown **80** Virginia Lee Burton

Photographers: 28 Susan Lapides **29** Bob Daemmrich/Stock Boston **30** Gabe Palmer/Stock Market **31** Joel Gordon **32** Bill Frantz/Click/Chicago **33** Peter Pearson/Click/Chicago **34** Rothwell/FPG **35** Elyse Lewin/Image Bank **36** D. Hallinan/FPG **37** Bob Thomason/Leo DeWys, Inc. **38** David Phillips **39** D. Hallinan/FPG **40** David Lissy/Leo DeWys, Inc. **41** Comstock **42** James Kirby/Focus VA **43** Stockphotos

IJ-D-96543210

Contents

Good Ideas

Houghton Mifflin Literature
Mike Mulligan and His Steam Shovel

Good Ideas

Pumpkin Pumpkin

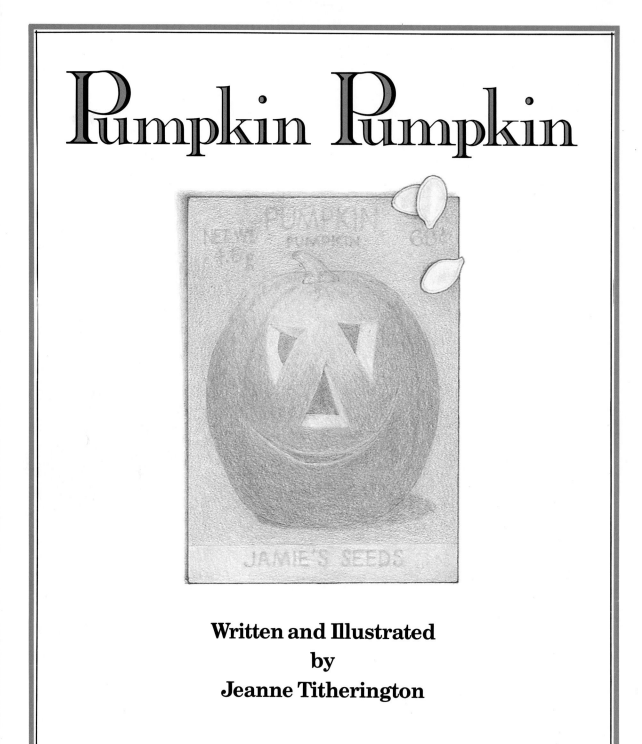

Written and Illustrated
by
Jeanne Titherington

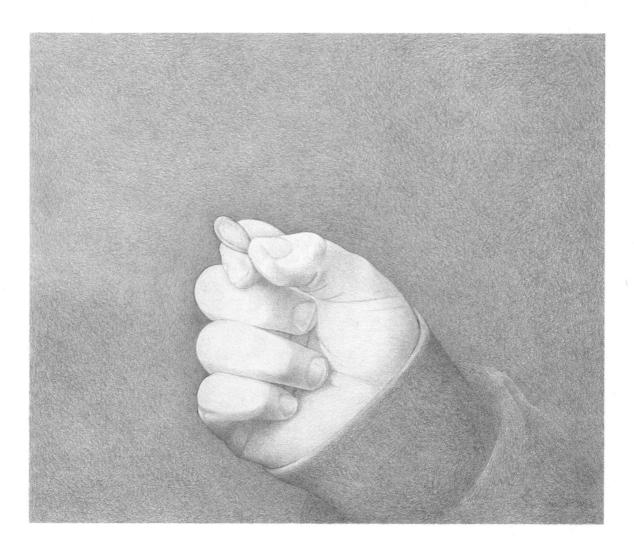

Jamie planted a pumpkin seed,

and the pumpkin seed
grew a pumpkin sprout,

and the pumpkin sprout
grew a pumpkin plant,

and the pumpkin plant
grew a pumpkin flower,

and the pumpkin flower
grew a pumpkin.

And the pumpkin grew . . .

and grew . . .

and grew,

until Jamie picked it.

Then Jamie scooped out
the pumpkin pulp,
carved a pumpkin face,
and put it in the window.
But . . .

he saved
six pumpkin seeds
for planting in the spring.

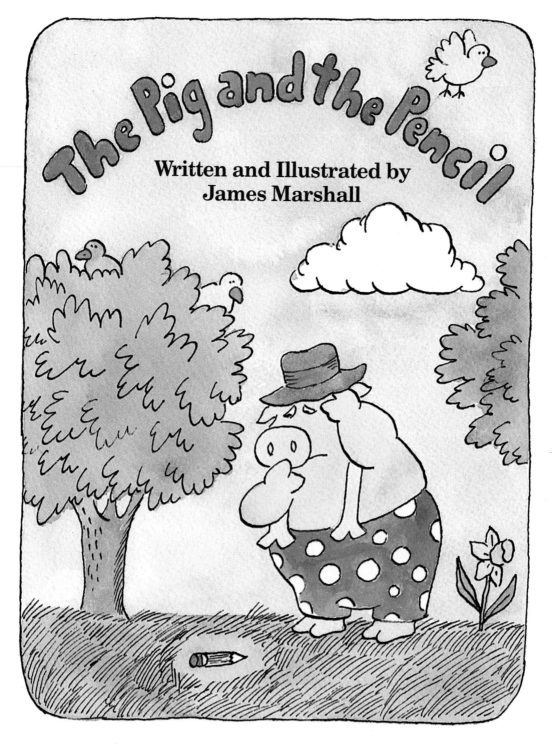

The Pig and the Pencil

**Written and Illustrated by
James Marshall**

Pig was looking at something on the ground. Turtle came by.

"What did you find, Pig?" she said. "What is that thing on the ground?"

"Don't you know?" said Pig.

"No, but you're smart. Can't you tell me what it is?" said Turtle.

"I'll do more than that," said Pig. "I'll <u>show</u> you what it is!"

Pig put the pencil on his hat.

"Oh, now I see!" said Turtle. "It looks good on your hat. You are so smart, Pig."

"I know, I know," said Pig.

Frog came by just then.

"Oh, Frog! Look what Pig put
on his hat," said Turtle.

"I see," said Frog. "That makes your
hat look good, Pig. What a smart thing
to do!"

"Being smart is what I do best," said
Pig. "Now I'll show you something more!"

Pig put the pencil on his nose.

"What a good place for it!" said Frog.

"I think that's the best place," said
Turtle. "You are so smart, Pig."

"I'll show you something more!" said Pig.

"What more can there be?" said
Turtle.

Pig jumped up and down with
the pencil on his nose.

"What a big jump!" said Frog.

"What a smart pig!" said Turtle.

Then Fox came by. She was looking
at the ground.

"Come here, Fox," said Pig. "Come
and see what I'm doing."

Fox said, "I can't, Pig. I am
looking for my pencil. Do you see it?"

"I don't think so," said Pig. "What's
a pencil?"

Fox looked at Pig's nose.
"There's my pencil!" she said.

"Where? Where?" said Pig. "I don't
see it."

"My pencil is on your nose!" said Fox.
"What's it doing there?"

"Don't you know?" said Turtle.
"That's the best place to put it!"

"No, no, no!" said Fox. "Pencils don't go on noses. That's not smart."

Fox took the pencil. She made pictures and letters.

"Look at what Fox is doing!" said Frog. "Now that's smart!"

"Pig, you didn't show us that," said
Turtle. "Did you forget?"

"Forget?" said Pig. "Yes, Turtle,
that's it! I think I did forget."

Water is Wet

by Penny Pollock

You can do lots of things with
water — drink it, play in it,
and let it dribble down your cheek.

You can pour water with a hose

or paint it with a brush.

You can smack water with your boot,

whack it with a stick,
or plunk it with a rock.

Water is handy for washing your dog,

scrubbing your pretend baby's
top and bottom, and bathing
your real baby, too.

Water is fine for helping things grow.

Water is great for making light bubbles

and heavy mud pies.

Rain is water from the sky.
It "pings" your umbrella
and tickles your fingers.

When winter rain turns into snow,
skiing and sledding are the way to go.

Anyone you know?

When frozen water turns to ice,
gliding on skates can be nice.

Water is grand for jumping,
flopping, and floating, too.
Water is wet — and wonderful.

Happiness

by A. A. Milne

John had
Great Big
Waterproof
Boots on;
John had a
Great Big
Waterproof
Hat;
John had a
Great Big
Waterproof
Mackintosh —
And that
(Said John)
Is
That.

Boo Bear Takes a Rest

**Written and Illustrated by
David McPhail**

Boo Bear helped Mother and Father
all morning.

"You have worked hard, Boo," said
Father. "Now it's time for a rest."

"I don't need a rest," said Boo.

"Little bears need to rest," said Mother, and she put Boo to bed. "Try to get some rest now."

"I don't think I need to rest," Boo said. "But I'll try, Mother."

"That's a good bear!" said Mother. "A little rest will do you good."

Father came in with some soup.
"Are you resting, Boo?" he asked.

"I'm trying my best," said Boo.

"Here's some nice soup for you," said
Father. "It will help you rest."

"Thank you, Father," said Boo.
"I need all the help I can get."

Then Pig came by. "It's not bedtime!"
he said. "What are you doing in bed?"

"I worked hard this morning," said
Boo. "Now I'm trying to rest."

"It's a good thing I'm here," said Pig.
"I'll play my horn for you. My playing
will help you rest."

"Thank you, Pig," said Boo. "I need
all the help I can get."

Then Frog came by. "It's not bedtime!" she said. "What are you doing in bed?"

"I worked hard this morning," said Boo. "Now I'm trying to rest. Pig is helping me."

"I'll help, too," said Frog. "Pig can play his horn, and I'll sing!"

"Thank you, Frog," said Boo. "I need all the help I can get."

Then Fox came by. "Boo!" she said.
"What's going on in here?"

"I worked hard this morning," said
Boo. "Now I'm trying to rest. Pig and
Frog are helping me."

"No one can rest in here, Boo," said
Fox. "Not with all this playing and
singing! Stop, Pig! Stop, Frog!"

Pig and Frog stopped.

"That's more like it," said Fox.

Boo said, "Can you help me, Fox?"

"Yes, I can," said Fox. "I'll read to you. A bedtime book will help you rest."

"Read to Frog and me, too," said Pig. "We need some rest now. Playing and singing is hard work!"

Pig, Frog, and Boo liked the book.

"Did my reading help you rest, Boo?" asked Fox.

"Yes, Fox. I'm all rested now," said Boo. "You helped Pig and Frog rest, too! You have worked hard, Fox. Now I think you need a rest!"

"Thank you, Boo. I do," said Fox.

Boo went out to help Father and
Mother.

"I had a nice rest," said Boo.
"My friends helped me. They worked
hard."

"They did?" asked Mother. "Where
are your friends now?"

"They are all in my bed," said Boo.
"Now <u>they</u> need a rest. Helping
someone rest is hard work!"

MY NEW BOY

by Joan Phillips
Illustrated by Lynn Munsinger

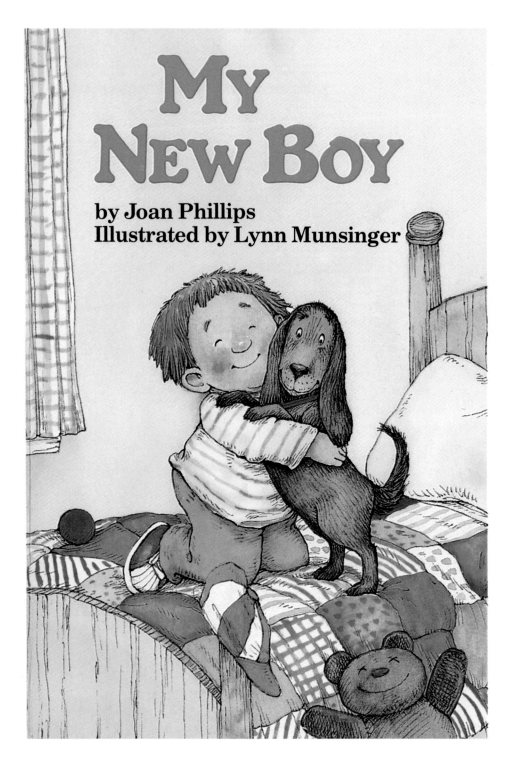

I am a little black puppy.
I live in a pet store.
Soon I will have a kid of my own.

Many kids come.
This one pulls my tail.
This one kisses too much.
They are not for me.

Here is another kid.
He says hello.
He pats my head.
Woof! Woof!
This is the boy for me!
My new boy takes me home.

I start taking care
of my boy right away.
I help him eat dinner.
I keep him clean.

I teach him to play tug of war.

I teach him to throw a ball to me.

I show my boy tricks.
I sit up. I roll over.

I teach my boy
to give me a bone
every time I do a trick.

My boy is not good
at everything.
He can not dig very fast.
He can not scratch his ears
with his foot.

He can not hide
under the bed.

My boy can not run
as fast as I can.
I run and run.
Oh, no! I do not see
my boy.
Is he lost?

I look behind a tree.
I look on the rocks.
I do not see my boy.

Is he on the swing? No.
Is he on the slide? No.
I do not see my boy
anywhere.

Now I see my boy.

He sees me too.

He is happy I found him.

We go home.
Woof! Woof! Woof!
I tell my boy he must not
get lost again.

My boy is lucky to have
a smart puppy like me!

Mr. Robot

by Laurene Krasny Brown
Illustrated by Marc Brown

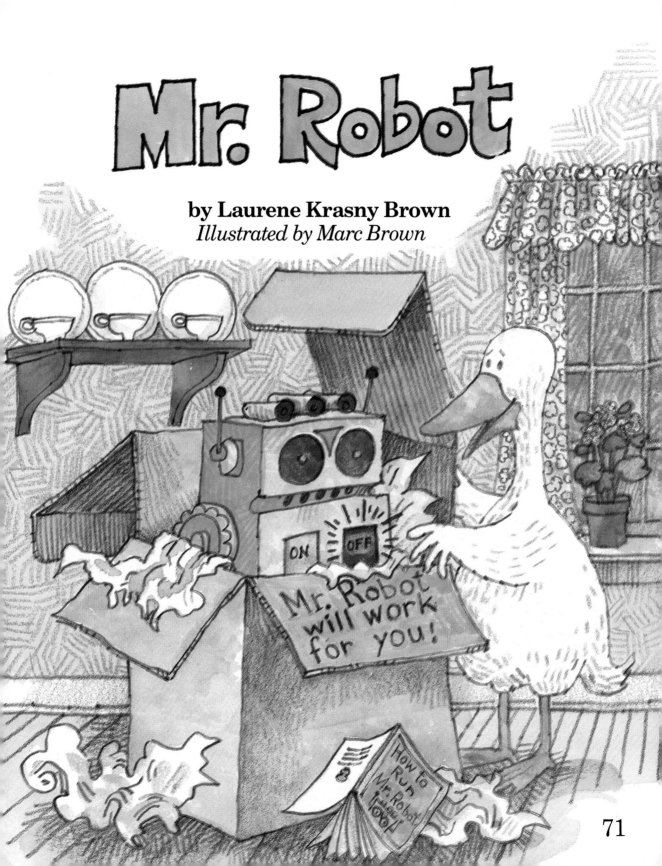

"Come in, Bear!" said Duck.
"You're just in time for lunch."

"What do you have here, Duck?"
asked Bear.

"This is Mr. Robot!" said Duck.
"He's going to work for me. He will
make a nice lunch for us.
Mr. Robot, go get lunch."

"I like Mr. Robot," said Bear.
"He can make lunch for me anytime!
May I please have a little more?"

"You may have all you want, Bear,"
Duck said. "Go, Mr. Robot. Bring
Bear some more lunch."

"This is fun, Duck!" said Bear.
"Mr. Robot makes a good lunch."

"Would you like some more?"
asked Duck.

"Oh, no thank you," said Bear.
"I have had much too much lunch!"

Duck said, "You may go now, Mr.
Robot. We don't need any more lunch."

"Duck!" said Bear. "Look at Mr.
Robot now. He's bringing us some soup!"

"No, Mr. Robot!" said Duck.
"I didn't ask you to bring us soup.
We don't want any more lunch!"

"Duck!" said Bear. "Look at Mr.
Robot now. He's bringing us <u>more</u> lunch!"

"Oh, no! Oh, no!" said Duck.
"Why are you doing this, Mr. Robot?
You are bringing too much!
We don't want any more lunch!"

"Help! Help!" said Bear. "Mr. Robot
is bringing us more and more lunch!
We have no place to put it all!
Do something, Duck!"

"I'm trying to," said Duck.
"But I don't know what to do!
I can't get Mr. Robot to stop!
Please stop, Mr. Robot! Stop!"

"You did it, Duck, you did it!"
said Bear. "Mr. Robot stopped!"

"Yes, I did it," said Duck. "But
how did I get Mr. Robot to stop?"

"You did it with one little word,"
said Bear. "That word is STOP!"

"Oh, now I see!" said Duck.
"STOP is a word I won't forget!"

"Look at all this lunch, Duck."
said Bear. "What can we do with it?"

"I know what we can do," said Duck.
"We'll ask some friends to come in.
They'll find a place for all this lunch!"

≈ *Houghton Mifflin Literature* ≈

Think of all the good ideas you
have read about in this book!
Now read about Mike Mulligan
and his steam shovel, Mary Anne.
Find out why they need a good idea.